YOUR KNOWLEDGE HAS VALUE

Christian Krogmann

Decarbonisation in Transport and Warehousing

Technological and behavioural opportunities

GRIN Verlag

Bibliografische Information der Deutschen Nationalbibliothek:

Die Deutsche Bibliothek verzeichnet diese Publikation in der Deutschen National-
bibliografie; detaillierte bibliografische Daten sind im Internet über http://dnb.d-
nb.de/ abrufbar.

Imprint:

Copyright © 2012 GRIN Verlag GmbH
Druck und Bindung: Books on Demand GmbH, Norderstedt Germany
ISBN: 978-3-656-21177-8

This book at GRIN:

http://www.grin.com/en/e-book/195085/decarbonisation-in-transport-and-warehou-
sing

GRIN - Your knowledge has value

Der GRIN Verlag publiziert seit 1998 wissenschaftliche Arbeiten von Studenten, Hochschullehrern und anderen Akademikern als eBook und gedrucktes Buch. Die Verlagswebsite www.grin.com ist die ideale Plattform zur Veröffentlichung von Hausarbeiten, Abschlussarbeiten, wissenschaftlichen Aufsätzen, Dissertationen und Fachbüchern.

Visit us on the internet:

http://www.grin.com/

http://www.facebook.com/grincom

http://www.twitter.com/grin_com

Heriot-Watt University

School of Management and Languages

MSc Logistics and Supply Chain Management

COURSE ASSIGNMENT 2012

Module Title:	Green Logistics
Module Code:	C11GL
Name:	Christian Krogmann
Word Count:	1999 (excl. references)

TABLE OF CONTENTS

LIST OF ABBREVIATIONS

BTL .... Biomass to Liquid

CO_2 .... Carbon dioxide

EU .... European Union

HVO .... Hydrogenated Vegetable Oil

IPCC .... Intergovernmental Panel on Climate Change

LED .... Light-emitting diode

UNEP .... United Nations Environment Programme

UNFCCC .... United Nations Framework Convention on Climate Change

WMO .... World Meteorological Organization

WTW .... Well-to-Wheel

LIST OF FIGURES

1 INTRODUCTION

The debate of climate change is occupying many parties not only in environmental terms and it has gained importance in the last decade. Although the existence of climate change and particularly a corresponding human responsibility has advocates and opponents, it is obvious that climate change will be a serious issue for everyone if it impacts our nature as predicted (IPCC, 2007a). Hence, institutions such as the IPPC, UNEP, WMO or UNFCCC were introduced in order to guide governments and principally everyone in order to assess and to mitigate climate change. The UNFCCC's ultimate aim, for instance, is to stabilize the concentration of greenhouse gases 'at a level that would prevent dangerous anthropogenic interference with the climate system' (United Nations, 1992: 9). However, this ultimate aim relies on many-sided sub-ordinate targets. One of these targets is to reduce carbon emissions in the logistics sector (McKinnon et al., 2010).

In the following chapter 2, opportunities for technological and behavioural changes in order to cut carbon emissions are presented for the logistical activities freight transport (main focus is on road transport) and warehousing. In chapter 3, an evaluation of the question which set of changes is likely to have greater influence is given together with a final conclusion.

2 DECARBONISATION STRATEGIES IN LOGISTICS

At least since the increasing importance of climate change, companies have to be aware of possible effects on their business. 'Climate change is likely to become a major business driver over the next few decades as companies come under intense pressure to decarbonise their activities' (McKinnon, 2010: 1). Hence, the main question is not whether companies are willing to decarbonise their activities but how they can implement their decarbonisation strategies into their business.

The other side of the coin is, however, that logistics activities derive from a primary demand for products and services (Cole, 2005). Consequently, companies offering logistics activities may not always have a lock on decarbonisation. To illustrate this point one need only refer to an exemplified case in which a customer demands a fast transportation leading to an airfreight shipment. Although a sea freight shipment would save relative carbon emissions, the logistics company would need to fulfil the customer's requirement if it did not want to dissatisfy the customer. Thus, decarbonisation might also be a question of weak or strong sustainability (Whitelegg, 1995), i.e. the trade-off of environmental against social or economic objectives or 'the imposition of environmental controls regardless of their economic and social consequences' (McKinnon et al., 2010: 342).

Nevertheless, the amount of CO_2 emissions is expected to grow as more carbon-intensive modes of transport gain greater proportions within the modal split (IPCC, 2007b). Hence, in order to fulfil the aim of stabilising carbon emissions, companies have to search and develop opportunities to reduce such emissions.

2.1   Freight Transport

Freight transport is a carbon-intensive sector. 'In 2004, transport was responsible for 23% of world energy-related GHG emissions with about three quarters coming from road vehicles' (IPCC, 2007b: 325). Additionally, the demand for freight transport is expected to grow robustly in the next decades (IPCC, 2007b; Sbihi and Eglese, 2007; Woodburn et al., 2008). Figure 1 also illustrates that freight transport including different modes accounts for the majority of carbon emissions within the logistics sector. Hence, it can be estimated that the biggest potential for CO_2 reduction is carried there.

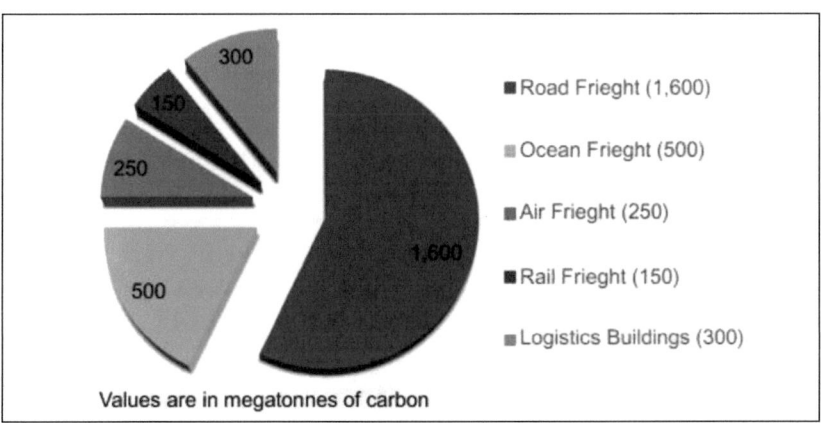

Figure 1: GHG Emissions per Logistics and Transport Activity
Source: Dey, LaGuardia and Srinivasan (2011)

Figure 2 gives a general overview about opportunities to reduce carbon emissions. Furthermore, determinants and corresponding outputs are illustrated.

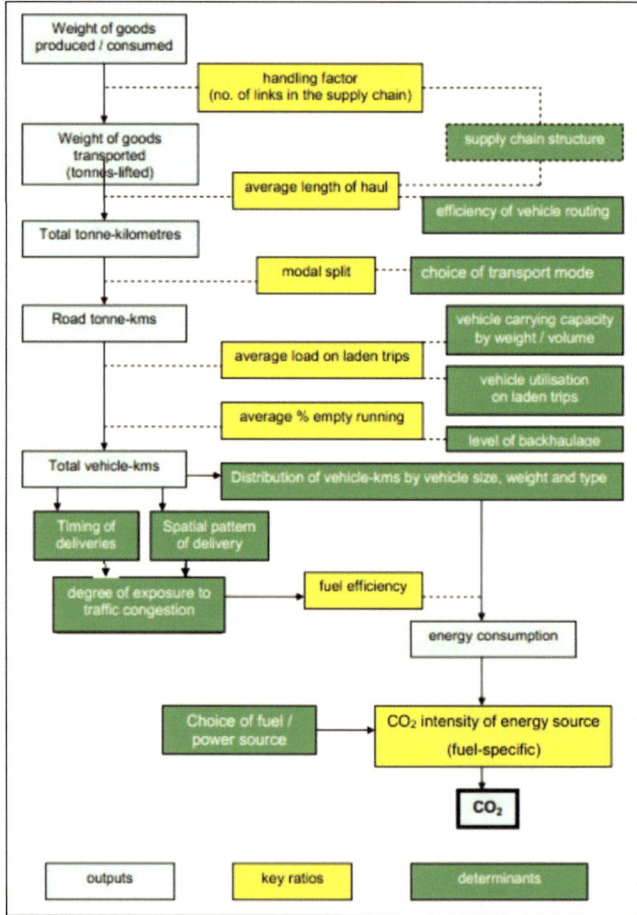

Figure 2: Framework for Analysing Opportunities for CO₂ Reduction
Source: McKinnon (2007)

However, the mentioned key ratios in figure 2 are not separated into technological and behavioural opportunities.

2.1.1   *Technological Opportunities*

An efficient way to reduce carbon emissions would be to undertake technological changes of vehicles. In this context, an increased carrying capacity is one opportunity (McKinnon et al., 2010). This can either be done in terms of weight reduction or volume augmentation. The advantage of higher carrying capacity is, on the one hand, a greater payload of vehicles. Consequently, fewer vehicles would be needed for the same amount of cargo transported and hence, a reduction in CO_2, expressed on a load-kilometres per litre basis, can be realized. The IPCC (2007b) and The Carbon Trust (2012) also identify reduction of loads as one opportunity for lower carbon emissions. On the other hand, McKinnon et al. (2010) state that increasing the carrying capacity reduce the fuel efficiency, expressed on a vehicle-kilometres per litre basis, although this expression is declared as less important.

However, these figures can also be improved by increasing energy efficiency, which is a second way to reduce carbon emissions (IPCC, 2007b; McKinnon et al., 2010). In this context, one has to distinguish between behavioural and technological actions to increase energy efficiency. Regarding technological actions, improving engine and exhaust systems are a main opportunity (McKinnon et al., 2010). In this connection, Baker et al. (2009) and The Carbon Trust (2012) present further examples. Baker et al. (2009: 24) classify the technological improvements into the groups 'vehicles', 'powertrains' and 'fuel'. Improvements for vehicles consist of advanced aerodynamics, i.e. customisation of the vehicle's chassis as well as advanced rolling resistance, i.e. use of special tyres. Adjustments such as aerodynamic trailers, trailer fairings or spray reduction mud flaps enable a CO_2 benefit that is estimated to be around 13.6% to 20% (Baker et al., 2009). Power train (drive train) technologies can also serve to reduce carbon emissions (IPCC, 2007b). In this context, Baker et al. (2009) identify combustion systems, friction reduction methods, engine accessories and gas exchange methods as key themes. Furthermore, they classify further drive train technologies such as waste heat recovery, alternative power trains (electric and cell vehicles), hybrid technology and transmission modifications as potential changes. Each group of modification has different saving potential (Baker et al., 2009).

The third category of Baker et al. (2009), also supported by others (IPCC, 2007b; Dey, LaGuardia and Srinivasan, 2011), is the change to less carbon intensive fuels such as BTL or HVO fuel. These fuels can save a huge amount of carbon emissions up to 90% on a WTW basis (Baker et al., 2009). Alternative fuels or biofuels also become increasingly important in the near future (Dey, LaGuardia and Srinivasan, 2011). McKinnon et al. (2010) and the World Economic Forum (2009) also identify clean vehicle technologies as a major part of technological opportunities. However, research must be conducted before these fuels become marketable (Baker et al., 2009).

To sum up one cannot deny that in the near future (up to 2020) technological improvements are an effective way to reduce carbon emissions if they can get marketable.

2.1.2 Behavioural Opportunities

Behaviour with respect to decarbonisation is likely to be even more important in the short term than technology. In order to gain CO_2 reductions, nothing needs to be invented but only behaviour has to be adapted. As already mentioned in the beginning of this chapter, decarbonisation is a question of strong or weak sustainability, too (McKinnon et al., 2010). Hence, the general willing to save carbon emissions must be existent.

Baker et al. (2009) identify changing driver behaviour as one key element to reduce carbon emissions. With help of corresponding trainings, drivers should be cultivated in order to drive more economical. In this context, companies can motivate their drivers by providing awards for efficient driving (McKinnon et al., 2010). Baker et al. (2009) number the potential GHG savings with 10% on average. On the other hand, it is important to retrain drivers continuously as effectiveness of economical driving is expected to fall off after a period of time.

The World Economic Forum (2009) also identified several behavioural saving options. Slowing down the movements of supply chains is one option with high saving potential. The biggest opportunity can be realized by slowing down ship movements because of 'the squared relationship between speed and emissions' (World Economic Forum, 2009: 17). But also road vehicle speed reductions and load fill improvements are efficient ways to decarbonise the supply chain.

Another possibility is the optimisation of networks (Sbihi and Eglese, 2007; World Economic Forum, 2009). Two big problems concerning networks are the relatively big proportion of movements running empty (24% of vehicle-kilometres in the EU) and the suboptimal utilisation of the vehicles' gross weights (57% of maximum gross weight on average) (World Economic Forum, 2009). Network optimisations are not only applicable to road transport. For example, aviation can also profit from improved operational efficiency by optimising routes, increasing utilisation or improving traffic management.

Modal switches are also an opportunity for CO_2 reductions. If companies want to reduce their carbon emissions, they will have to try to switch from carbon-intensive modes of transport to less carbon-intensive ones. The crucial aspect is the amount of emissions per tonne-kilometre (World Economic Forum, 2009). Therefore, useful changes are, for example, changes from intercontinental air to sea freight, short distance airfreight to road freight or long distance road transport to rail or inland waterway transports (World Economic Forum, 2009).

Another carbon-friendly alternative would be the shift from offshoring to nearshoring, although the CO_2 benefit would be relatively small. Relative carbon inefficiency of land transportation compared to sea freight is the main reason for this (World Economic Forum, 2009). However, transport distances and tonne-kilometres would decrease significantly and hence, contribute to the reduction of carbon emissions.

2.2   Warehousing

Warehousing as another key logistics activity can also contribute to mitigate climate change by reducing carbon emissions. Figure 3 shows the energy use split in typical warehouses.

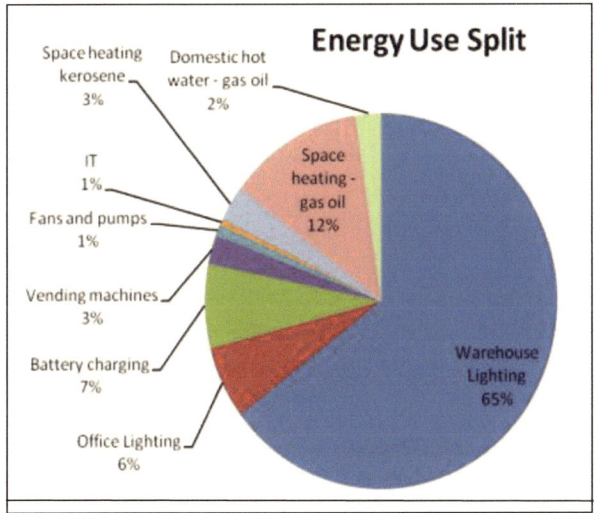

Figure 3: Energy Use Split of an average sized warehouse (15,000 m²)
Source: UK Warehousing Association (2010)

It is observable that the energy is primarily used for lighting of a warehouse. Heating comes in the second place. However, McKinnon (2010) identifies heating as responsible for the majority of energy used. Regardless of the rank order, the figure shows that biggest potential can be found in lighting and heating.

2.2.1   *Technological Opportunities*

Different authors focus on energy efficiency as the main aspect for technological opportunities (IPCC, 2007b; McKinnon, 2010; The Carbon Trust, 2008; World Economic Forum, 2009). Dalton (2009) states that a significant reduction in carbon emissions can be realized by 'reducing the demand for heating through good insulation and airtight construction methods and reducing the need for artificial light by increasing the use of daylight supplemented by energy-efficient lighting systems'. This sentence shows the multitude of possibilities that can be realised in terms of better energy efficiency. To illustrate this point one need only refer to the technology of LEDs. These are '1000 times more efficient than a kerosene lamp' (IPCC, 2007b: 402). McKinnon (2010) adds that installing wind turbines or solar panels are also a possibility to reduce carbon emissions. Undoubtedly, the use of renewable energy sources avoids the use of fossil energy and is thus, carbon-friendly. Finally, internal warehouse operations such as order picking, or transporting via fork lift trucks can also be designed more carbon-friendly by using corresponding technologies such as paperless operations or electric engines (Rushton, Croucher and Baker, 2010).

2.2.2 *Behavioural Opportunities*

Besides technological opportunities, reduction of carbon emissions can also be achieved by a corresponding ecology-minded behaviour. Franchetti et al. (2009) identify inventory control as one possibility. Keeping a reasonable stock level on hand can avoid the need for bigger warehouses. Certainly, smaller warehouses lead to less energy expended and hence to less emissions.

Another way is simply the reduction of the number of warehouses in the network. CO_2 emissions can be cut by returning to a more decentralised warehousing system as this avoids movements (McKinnon, 2008). The other side of the coin is, however, that this leads to increased inventory and warehousing costs.

There is no doubt that training and communication is also an issue for reducing carbon emissions in warehousing. People should be advised to behave in a carbon-friendly way which can be realised by corresponding building efficiency trainings. This behaviour also includes the attitude to recycling (World Economic Forum, 2009).

3 DISCUSSION AND CONCLUSION

The previous chapter showed different opportunities for reducing carbon emissions separated into technological and behavioural ones. The question is whether their impact can also be separated consequently. Verbeek and Slob (2006: 5) point out that 'in environmental policy, attention is focused either on the development and promotion of clean technologies [...] or on stimulating environmentally-friedly behaviour'. However, they also state that there should be an integrated approach. It is difficult to evaluate which set of changes will have greater impact as they are also directly connected. Introduction of new technologies in a company always have to do with their behaviour with respect to a corresponding implementation. As previously mentioned, companies have to respond to the question whether they want strong or weak sustainability. Moreover, it depends on the progress of research and development of new technologies and, undoubtedly, on the capital available for technological investments. The time to market is also difficult to estimate for several technologies. Against this background, behavioural changes might rather be realisable than technological ones over the time-scale 2012-2020.

However, it is important to mention that the reduction of carbon emissions does not only rely on freight transport and warehousing. Technologies and behaviour with regard to production are just as important as packaging design, information flows or purchasing and hence, they also have to be considered for the aim to reduce carbon emissions (Dey, LaGuardia and Srinivasan, 2011; World Economic Forum, 2009).

LIST OF REFERENCES

Baker, H., Cornwell, R., Koehler, E. and Patterson, J. (2009) *Review of Low Carbon Technologies for Heavy Goods Vehicles*, Report prepared by Ricardo for the Department for Transport, London.

Cole, S. (2005) *Applied Transport Economics: Policy, Management & Decision Making*, 3rd edition, London: Kogan Page.

Dalton, M. (2009) 'Take the green route out of the red', *SupplyChainStandard* [online], 5 May, Available from: http://www.supplychainstandard.com/Articles/2344/Take+the+green+route+out+of+the+red.html (Accessed 14 March 2012).

Dey, A., LaGuardia, P. and Srinivasan, M. (2011) 'Building sustainability in logistics operations: a research agenda', *Management Research Review*, vol. 34, no. 11, pp. 1237-1259.

Franchetti, M., Bedal, K., Ulloa, J. and Grodek, S. (2009) 'Lean and Green: Industrial engineering methods are natural stepping stones to green engineering', *Industrial Engineer*, vol. 41, no. 9, pp. 24-29.

IPCC (2007a) *Climate Change 2007: Impacts, Adaption and Vulnerability*, Cambridge: Cambridge University Press.

IPCC (2007b) *Climate Change 2007: Mitigation of Climate Change*, Cambridge: Cambridge University Press.

McKinnon, A. (2007) *CO_2 Emissions from Freight Transport in the UK*, Report prepared for the Climate Change Working Group of the Commission of Integrated Transport, London.

McKinnon, A. (2008) *The Potential of Economic Incentives to Reduce CO_2 Emissions from Goods Transport*, Paper prepared for the 1st International Transport Forum on 'Transport and Energy: the Challenge of Climate Change', Leipzig.

McKinnon, A. (2010) 'Green Logistics: The Carbon Agenda', *LogForum*, vol. 6, iss. 3, no. 1.

McKinnon, A., Cullinane, S., Browne, M. and Whiteing, A. (ed.) (2010) *Green Logistics: Improving the environmental sustainability of logistics*, London: Kogan Page.

Rushton, A., Croucher, P. and Baker, P. (ed.) (2010) *The Handbook of Logistics & Distribution Management*, London: Kogan Page.

Sbihi, A. and Eglese, R.W. (2007) *The Relationship between Vehicle Routing & Scheduling and Green Logistics - A Literature Survey* [online], Green Logistics WM6 Report, Lancaster, Available from: http://www.greenlogistics.org/SiteResources/WM6-Lancaster-VehicleRoutingandScheduling.pdf (Accessed 14 March 2012).

The Carbon Trust (2008) *Low Carbon Refurbishment of Buildings: A guide to achieving carbon savings from refurbishment of non-domestic buildings*, London: The Carbon Trust.

The Carbon Trust (2012) *Transport* [online], Available from: http://www.carbontrust.co.uk/emerging-technologies/technology-directory/Pages/Transport.aspx (Accessed 14 March 2012).

UK Warehousing Association (2010) *Save Energy, Cut Costs: Energy Efficient Warehouse Operation*, London: UK Warehousing Association.

United Nations (1992) *United Nations Framework Convention on Climate Change* [online], Bonn: United Nations, Available from: http://unfccc.int/files/essential_background/background_publications_htmlpdf/application/pdf/conveng.pdf (Accessed 11 March 2012).

Verbeek, P.-P. and Slob, A. (2006) *User Behaviour and Technology Development: Shaping Sustainable Relations Between Consumers and Technologies*, Dordrecht: Springer.

Whitelegg, J. (1995) *Freight Transport, Logistics and Sustainable Development*, London: World Wide Fund for Nature.

Woodburn, A., Allen, J., Browne, M. and Leonardi, J. (2008) *The Impacts of Globalisation on International Road and Rail Freight Transport activity: Past trends and future perspectives*, Guadalajara: Global Forum on Transport and Environment in a Globalising World.

World Economic Forum (2009) *Supply Chain Decarbonization: The Role of Logistics and Transport in Reducing Supply Chain Carbon Emissions* [online], Geneva: World Economic Forum, Available from: http://www3.weforum.org/docs/WEF_LT_SupplyChainDecarbonization_Report_2009.pdf (Accessed 12 March 2012).